Jesus and the Last Things

Jesus and the Last Things

Death, Judgment, Heaven, Hell

Dennis J. Billy, CSsR

WIPF & STOCK · Eugene, Oregon

JESUS AND THE LAST THINGS
Death, Judgment, Heaven, Hell

Copyright © 2019 Dennis J. Billy, CSsR. All rights reserved. Except for brief quotations in critical publications or reviews, no part of this book may be reproduced in any manner without prior written permission from the publisher. Write: Permissions, Wipf and Stock Publishers, 199 W. 8th Ave., Suite 3, Eugene, OR 97401.

Wipf & Stock
An Imprint of Wipf and Stock Publishers
199 W. 8th Ave., Suite 3
Eugene, OR 97401

www.wipfandstock.com

PAPERBACK ISBN: 978-1-5326-8168-4
HARDCOVER ISBN: 978-1-5326-8169-1
EBOOK ISBN: 978-1-5326-8170-7

Manufactured in the U.S.A.   MAY 17, 2019

Versions of material in this book have appeared elsewhere under the following titles: "The Cross in God: A Lenten Meditation," *The Priest* 61 (2005) 37–39; "The 'Many Dwelling Places' of Jesus' Farewell Discourse," *Pastoral Life* 53 (2004) 23–28; "Putting Last Things First: Meditation and the Ethics of Eschatology," *Pastoral Life* 54 (2005) 30–37; "Reaching the Alienated Heart: An Interpretation of Jesus' Descent into Hell," *Review for Religious* 64 (2005) 118–28; "Towards Deep Heaven: The Last Judgment and Catholic Imagination," *Review for Religious* 63 (2004) 342–51.

All quotations from Scripture in the book come from *Holy Bible: New Revised Standard Version with Apocrypha*. New York: Oxford University Press, 1989.

In fond memory of
Jonathan Scott

(1946–2018)

Both in life and in death we are the Lord's. That is why Christ died and came to life again, that he might be Lord of both the dead and the living.

—Rom 14:8–9

Contents

Introduction / ix

1. The Death of Christ / 1
2. The Descent of Christ / 13
3. The Judgment of Christ / 25
4. The Destiny of Christ / 37
5. The Four Last Things / 47

   Conclusion / 59

Bibliography / 61

Introduction

CATHOLIC SPIRITUALITY HAS TRADITIONALLY placed a great deal of emphasis on the importance of meditating on the four last things: death, judgment, heaven, and hell. It does so in order to help us be aware of the transitory nature of our lives on earth and to remind us that our actions on this side of death have much to do with the shaping of our eternal destiny. Meditation on the last things, we are told, enables us to focus on the one thing that matters: our relationship with Christ, our Lord.

Jesus has much to teach us about the four last things. He faced death with courage and was raised to new life by the power of his heavenly Father. He descended into hell and reached out to those who had alienated themselves from God. He promised to return at the consummation of time to judge the living and the dead and to establish the fullness of his kingdom. He lives forever in the house of his Father, hoping to draw all people to himself and make all things new. For him, the four last things are just a prelude to the first things. He is the Alpha and Omega, the beginning and the end. He teaches us to put last things first and first things last.

This book focuses on what Jesus teaches us about death, judgment, heaven, and hell. It examines the doctrine behind these four important assertions of the Catholic faith and seeks to find their relevance for our lives today. Chapter 1, "The Death of Christ," looks at Jesus's crucifixion and sees in it an expression of the humility of God and the

Introduction

divine self-emptying. Chapter 2, "The Descent of Christ," examines the meaning of Jesus's descent into hell and the significance it has for those who have willingly cut themselves off from the love of God. Chapter 3, "The Judgment of Christ," discusses the doctrine of the last judgment and its relevance for our actions in daily life. Chapter 4, "The Destiny of Christ," sees the glorious and risen Lord living in his Father's house, his heavenly home, and reigning as King of the new creation. Chapter 5, "The Four Last Things," shows how the church's teaching on the last things has important implications for how we conduct our lives. Each of these chapters concludes with a series of reflections, questions, and a brief prayer on the particular last thing in question. The conclusion, "Putting Last Things First," places the church's teaching on the last things in the wider context of Paul's teaching on love in his First Letter to the Corinthians.

Jesus is Lord of the living and the dead. He teaches us that love is stronger than death and that death itself will one day die. He reminds us that love, not chaos, underlies all reality and that those who refuse its gentle embrace will ultimately alienate themselves from God and linger for all eternity in the unreal, darkened shadows of loneliness and sin. It was C. S. Lewis who once wrote, "the gates of hell are locked on the *inside*."[1] If this be true, then the last things— death, judgment, heaven, hell— remind us that the truth about our lives will one day be fully revealed and that if we refused to receive the transforming grace of Christ in this life, we will fail to do so in the next.

---

1. Lewis, *Problem of Pain*, 127.

1

The Death of Christ

"Death has been swallowed up in victory." "Where, O death, is your victory? Where, O death, is your sting?" The sting of death is sin, and the power of sin is the law. But thanks be to God, who gives us the victory through our Lord Jesus Christ.

—1 COR 15:55–57

HARDLY ANYONE DISPUTES THE historical claim made in the Apostles' Creed that Jesus "suffered under Pontius Pilate, was crucified, died, and was buried."[1] This affirmation lies at the narrative heart of the Christian faith and provides the historical backdrop against which the events of Easter morning would unfold. Although they may differ in details, the Gospels are remarkably clear on who killed the carpenter of Nazareth and by whose direct order. This indisputable fact roots the Christian faith in history and gave early believers an important historical context for their ongoing reflection on the meaning of the Christ event.

1. *Roman Missal*, 511.

Death by Crucifixion

Crucifixion by the Romans took place publicly and in the open air. It began with stripping the criminal and scourging the criminal at the place of judgment. To shame him before the people, he was then forced to carry the crossbeam of the cross naked through the streets to the place of execution. Along the way he was mocked and often spat upon by those who lined the streets. If his strength appeared to be waning, someone was forced to carry the crossbeam for him so that he would not die before he reached the place of execution.

Once there, the naked criminal was fastened to the crossbeam by rope or by nail. He was then hoisted high in the air so that the crossbeam could rest either at the top of the vertical beam, which was permanently in place, or in a specially carved notch near the top. Above his head was placed an inscription listing the crime for which he was being executed. To augment his torments, the criminal's feet were usually fastened or nailed to a wooden support so that he would be able to breathe by pulling up from his arms and pushing down with his legs. If the legs were left dangling in the air, death would come much sooner.

When the Romans wanted to teach the people a special lesson, they raised the criminal very high in the air so that more would be able to see him. Death often took a matter of days. If the Romans were in a rush, they would hasten death by either breaking the criminal's legs or by piercing his side with a lance. The body would be left on the cross to rot. If it was close to the ground, it could even be torn apart and eaten by wild animals.

With a few notable exceptions, the accounts of Jesus's death closely resemble this routine pattern of Roman execution. The Jews had been given certain concessions by the Romans for executions taking place in Palestine.

Jesus, for example, was given back his clothing after being scourged because of objections about driving a criminal naked through the streets (Mark 15:20; Matt 27:31). In another concession to the Jews, he was offered some wine drugged with myrrh to numb the pain (Mark 15:23; Matt 27:34; John 19:29). His body, moreover, was not left to rot on the cross, but, in keeping with Jewish law (Deut 21:23), was taken down and buried before the end of the day (Mark 15:42–47).

Despite these few allowances, Jesus's death was horrible and excruciatingly painful. The Romans used crucifixion to break the criminal down physically, emotionally, socially, and even spiritually. In Jesus's day, it was a brutal reminder of Roman occupation and domination. Compared to crucifixion, stoning—the typical Jewish form of capital punishment—was relatively quick and painless. The Romans used fear to dominate the nations. Crucifixion was a principal tool in their repertoire, one that many feared and few had the courage to face, let alone endure. What happened to Jesus on Good Friday was exceedingly brutal but nothing unusual by Roman standards. If Pilate's order was routine and commonplace, however, Jesus's courageous embrace of death exceeded all human limits and brought the world to the threshold of the sacred.

The Cross in God

Why would Jesus embrace such horrific suffering? Did he do so freely? Was he moved by some kind of necessity? Could his death have been avoided? What does it mean for us? For centuries, Christians have asked themselves these and similar questions as they reflected upon the meaning of Jesus's passion and death. Although their answers vary in details and very often reflect their surrounding historical and cultural milieus, they almost always agree that he suffered and died to free us from our sins and to manifest God's unending love for us.

Horace Bushnell once said, "There is a cross in God before the wood is seen on Calvary."[2] Some people find such words enigmatic and difficult to accept. Suffering, after all, is not a goal to strive for, but something to put up with and eventually overcome. How could suffering exist in the very heart of God? The uneasy marriage between Greek and Hebrew thought from which early Christian theology was forged complicates the matter further. The Greek philosophers believed God was impassible (i.e., unchanging and, therefore, unfeeling) and identified him with the three transcendental values of the One, the True, and the Good. The Hebrew Scriptures, by way of contrast, evolved in their understanding of the divine and increasingly came up with a loving, all-powerful, and compassionate God actively engaged in the destiny of his people. Each of these conflicting understandings eventually found its way into the orthodox Christian presentation of the doctrine of God.

Christian theologians traditionally used the Greek approach when probing the nature of the Godhead, but followed the Hebrew point of view when reflecting upon God's involvement in human history. By juxtaposing these two very different understandings of divinity and insisting that both were valid representations of God's nature, they succeeded in preserving a deep sense of the mystery of who God was. By means of this "coincidence of opposites," God was recognized as the One, the True, and the Good, but also as the God of Abraham, Isaac, and Jacob. The church fathers believed that this very same God was humanity's Creator, Redeemer, and Sanctifier, a Trinity of divine persons sharing the same divine substance. They also believed

2. Bushnell, *Vicarious Sacrifice*, 35.

that Jesus Christ was the fullness of the God's revelation to humanity: "If you know me, you will know my Father also. From now on you do know him and have seen him" (John 14:7).

To say that there is a cross in God even before Jesus's death on Calvary takes the Christian understanding of God one step further and offers a profound insight into the mystery of God's inner life. "No one has greater love than this, to lay down one's life for one's friends" (John 15:13). Jesus's crucifixion was a defining moment of his life: it says something about who he was and what he stood for; it should also tell us something about his relationship to the Father.

That relationship, Christians believe, is rooted in the intimate bond of love they share by virtue of the Spirit, who proceeds from them. If God's very nature is defined by love, then the cross, as the symbol of love par excellence, *had* to be in God before the wood was seen on Calvary. The difficulty comes when we recognize that that very same cross is also a symbol of deep human anguish.

Can love and suffering be separated? Much depends on what we mean by the terms. There are different types of love just as there are different types of suffering. God's love is called charity (*caritas* in Latin; *agape* in Greek) and is associated with the selfless giving of oneself to another. In its human embodiment, it has been described by Thomas Aquinas as "a certain kind of friendship with God."[3]

In its most general sense, "suffering" typically means "enduring some kind of pain"— physical, psychological, spiritual, even social. If divine love can have a human embodiment, perhaps human suffering (or something like it) can also exist in God. After all, is not the human person created in God's own image and likeness? To love as God loves does not necessarily mean that one is going to "endure

3. Aquinas, *Summa Theologica* (2–2.23.5), 1266.

some kind of pain" for someone. It does imply, however, that one would be willing to do so should the need arise. That is precisely why the wood is seen on Calvary. Jesus's love is redemptive. There was a need for it.

The pain of God manifests itself in the divine self-emptying: "Let the same mind be in you that was in Christ Jesus, who, though he was in the form of God, did not regard equality with God something to be exploited, but emptied himself, taking the form of a slave, being born in human likeness" (Phil 2:5–7). Suffering in God occurs primarily in the will. God does not will to suffer; he suffers because he refuses to abandon humanity to the dark powers within it. Does God endure pain? "My Father, if this cannot pass unless I drink it, your will be done" (Matt 26:42). Who is suffering more here: the Son or the Father? Can the Father really be indifferent to the Son's pain? If so, what kind of Father would he be? Let there be no doubt, there was agony in God *before* the Son's agony in the garden and on the cross—and even *after*.

Jesus's death on the cross says something about his relationship with the Father and reveals to us something about the very nature of God. God has a heart—and it can be broken. He was willing to become one of us and die for us in order to manifest his love for us, mend our own hearts, and make us whole. Our God is a God of compassion; he suffers not only *for* us, but also *with* us. The real "coincidence of opposites" here is the way he brought together both the human and divine in the person of Jesus in order to embrace human experience and make it his own. Was there a cross in God before the wood was seen on Calvary? There certainly was. If not, Calvary would never have happened, and we would never have known the joy of God's friendship.

Through Jesus's death the cross, the symbol par excellence of Roman brutality and domination, was transformed into the distinctive symbol of a new religion. His testimony from the cross marks the beginning of this important change. A verse from the prophet Isaiah says it best: "They shall beat their swords into plowshares and their spears into pruning hooks" (Isa 2:4). Jesus teaches us how to do so. He encountered the cross—and embraced it. He responded to the violence of the Roman Empire with the silent message of a kingdom of another world. Through his death, he took an instrument of death and turned it into a lasting sign of hope and comfort for countless millions.

Some Further Insights

These reflections on Jesus's suffering and death invite further comment, if for no other reason than to draw out some of their implications for the belief and practice of the faith. The following remarks, while in no way exhaustive, seek to highlight some of the more relevant areas of practical application to the spiritual life.

Jesus's death at the hands of the Romans was one of the most painful and humiliating of deaths imaginable. This sort of public execution represented failure in the eyes of men and brought shame to the individual and those connected with him. At the time of his death, Jesus was deemed by nearly everyone a complete and utter failure. The hope he had inspired in his followers had completely dissipated; he had been left alone and literally suspended in the air to bleed profusely and eventually suffocate to death. In this moment of darkness, however, feeling abandoned by all, he still found the resources within himself to trust in the power of the Father's love. Jesus's death encourages us to look at our own failures and to face the shameful and humiliating moments of our lives with courage and quiet trust in God's promises.

Jesus's death on the cross was an act of selfless giving. Early on in his public ministry, he taught his disciples to love their enemies and to pray for their persecutors (Matt 5:44). As he hangs from the cross, he demonstrates that he lived what he taught—even in death. When he asks his Father to forgive his tormentors, he does so from a heart that within a short while would be pierced by the lance of one of the very men he was forgiving. By asking his Father to forgive, he teaches us that to hurt another person deliberately and unjustly is also a sin against God himself. As a result, the person who hurts another in this way ultimately hurts himself or herself in the process. This self-inflicted wound is what Jesus sees when he looks down from the cross and gazes upon his tormentors. Moved with compassion for them, he turns to his Father in heaven and intercedes on their behalf. He does the same for us whenever we injure ourselves in this way. Through his death, he takes our sins upon himself and pleads our cause.

Jesus's sense of abandonment embraced every dimension of his being: the physical, the emotional, the mental, the social, and especially the spiritual. In this tortured state, he entered the depths of our broken humanity and brought it back to wholeness. He did so by confronting the powers of darkness with the power of love. His death on the cross would ultimately show that love was stronger than death and formed the underlying fabric of reality. As he hung from the cross, however, all this remained mysteriously hidden from sight. Abandoned by his Father at this critical juncture of his life, he had one fundamental choice before him: to despair of life and of all he hoped for or to trust that, even though he seemed so distant and far away, the love of the Father would ultimately be there for him. Jesus chose the latter and never doubted his decision. Aided by his Spirit, he invites us to follow suit.

Jesus represents both God's gift to humanity and humanity's gift to God. As God's gift to humanity he is the Redeemer. Through his death on the cross, Jesus made humanity's fellowship with God once again possible. God's gift to us implies a need on our part. Jesus did for us something we were unable to do for ourselves. Because of our egoism and self-centeredness, it was impossible for us to rectify our relationship with God. Human nature had somehow gone awry, and only God himself could make it right again. Becoming human was God's way of straightening things out. By entering our world and becoming one of us, God was able to intercede for us on our behalf. Jesus continues to do so for us to this very day. He is our means to the Father, the path each of us must follow to pass from this life to life eternal.

In his dying moments from the cross, Jesus was not only giving himself as an offering of self to the Father. He was also giving himself to us. His passion and death stand as a model of courage for his followers to imitate. Down through the centuries, generation upon generation of Christians would look to the cross and see in the bloodied corpus hanging from it both a challenge and a call. The challenge would be to dare to trust in him as he trusted in the Father. The call would be to pick up their own crosses and follow in his steps. Jesus's cross is always challenging and calling us. No matter where we are, it stands as a reminder of someone who gave every ounce of his life for us in order that we might live. His challenge and his call ask us to do the same for others. Jesus's death on the cross seeks to evoke from us a similar response.

Jesus's suffering and death continue to this day in the members of his body. We who have been immersed in his paschal mystery participate in his suffering and death. We will be crucified on the crosses that we have shouldered for him and his following. We will suffer innocently from wounds inflicted upon our bodies and souls. The crucifix serves as a reminder of what Jesus went through for us and of what he is asking us to go through for him and for others. When we look at it, we are reminded that we too must face our suffering and eventual death with expectant apprehension, enduring patience, and steadfast perseverance. Our joy and zest for life will be tinged with the knowledge of a death that is to come. Our suffering in the moment will serve as a window to eternity, opening us up to the intimate life of the Godhead. Our focus on the reason and end of life will help us to face our suffering and death with steadfast perseverance. Because of Jesus's suffering and death, our own suffering and death take on new meaning. Through Christ, the power of God's love has been unleashed in the world. Jesus gives us the opportunity to share in that power and to be with him until our earthly end converges into his.

"Father, into your hands I commend my spirit" (Luke 23:46). When Jesus commends his spirit to the Father, he offers along with it the spirit of all humanity. In his final act of earthly freedom, he entrusts the human spirit—the vitality and lifeblood of the human race—to the Father's care. This act was something we could not do of our own accord. Someone had to do it for us, someone like us but also like God, someone human but also divine. In this final act, Jesus acts as the true mediator between God and man. He takes our place before God and intercedes for us. In his last words, he prays the prayer we longed to pray, but could not. He takes us with him as he faces death and places us with him in the Father's care. We face death together and, because we are in the Father's care, together shall overcome it. Jesus has identified himself so closely with humanity that

his story has become our story, and our story, his. Because of this close identity, we trust that he who suffered and died for us will be there for us in our time of need. Jesus identifies our needs with his needs. Anything we ask the Father in his name, we shall receive (John 15:16).

Conclusion

Jesus identified with us so closely that he bore on his shoulders the full weight of our human sinfulness. His innocence replaced our guilt; his nearness to the Father, the distance separating us from the divine. Jesus entered our world not to condemn it, but to save it (John 3:17). He did so by embracing death on our behalf so that our destiny could be inexorably bound up with his. His destiny was to live and die by the power of love, a force he unleashed on the world through his suffering and death on the cross.

Through the wood of the cross, Jesus defeated the power of death with the powerlessness of love. Although death had embraced Jesus by imprinting its cold, lifeless marks into his bloodied limbs and corpus, it could not subdue him, for he had overcome his fear of death and commended his spirit to his Father's care. That care would become our hope and the cause of our salvation. It would bind up our wounds and heal us our hearts. It would bring us back to health and lead us to new life. It would show us the way to the kingdom and enable us, with Jesus, to share in the riches of the Father's glory.

The triumph of the cross demonstrates the power of God's love for humanity. It celebrates Jesus's victory over death and marks a decisive defeat for evil's power to hold sway in our hearts. Just as Moses in the desert raised the serpent on a pole to heal all who cast their eyes upon it from the venomous poison within them (Num 21:4–9), so was

Jesus lifted up on the wood of the cross to bring eternal life to all who look to him in faith (John 3:14–15). Wandering through the desert with poison in one's veins is an apt description of the human situation. Moses gained healing for his people by interceding to God on their behalf. Jesus does the same and gains healing for us not from a single encounter with venomous snakes, but from death itself. Because of Jesus's death on the cross, the deadly poison flowing in our veins has been extracted; the antidote generously applied. On the wood of the cross, the selflessness of love struggled with the power of death—and proved victorious. Death was found seriously wanting and was eventually overcome.

Reflection Questions

- What does Jesus's passion and death tell us about God?
- What does it tell us about the human condition?
- What does it tell us about our own suffering and death?
- How does Jesus's suffering and death relate to our own?
- What difference does make for our own lives?

Prayer

Lord, you suffered and died so that I might live.
    Help me to live in hope and die with a living faith.

2

The Descent of Christ

When it says, "He ascended," what does it mean but that he had also descended into the lower parts of the earth? He who descended is the same one who ascended far above all the heavens, so that he might fill all things.

—Eph 4:9–10

The doctrine of Christ's descent into hell after his suffering and death on Good Friday conveys some very important truths about the meaning and scope of the paschal mystery. To understand this doctrine, we must distinguish between its theological formulation and the underlying truth it seeks to express. We must also put aside whatever prejudices we might have that will prevent us from probing this doctrine for its full worth and from opening our hearts to the deep spiritual wisdom it wishes to impart. My purpose in this chapter is to explore what the Apostles' Creed means when it says that "he [Jesus] descended into hell" and see how this teaching impacts our lives today.

Jesus and the Last Things

Christ's Redemptive Self-Emptying

To begin with, it is important to note that the descent into hell makes sense only if we examine it in the context of the Creed's other affirmations about Christ, especially those related to his plan of redemption. The Apostles' Creed, we are told ". . . is rightly considered to be a faithful summary of the apostles' faith" and constitutes "the oldest Roman catechism."[1] Since all of the church's teachings about Christ are closely related, just where this particular doctrine appears in the Creed can tell us much about its overall function in the faith of the early church. When looking at its immediate textual context, we see that Jesus's descent is strategically placed between affirmations about his suffering and death (i.e., "he suffered under Pontius Pilate, was crucified, died, and was buried.") and the proclamation of his resurrection ("On the third day he rose again."). If to enter the realm of the dead was considered by the early Christians to be a natural outcome of Jesus's passion and death, then rising from it victoriously necessarily preceded his glorious ascent into heaven. This immediate context tells us that Jesus's descent into hell occupies an important place in the overall narrative structure of Jesus's redemptive journey. If it did not, it would never have been placed at the very heart of the Creed's christological affirmations.

The larger textual context of the christological affirmations in the Apostles' Creed makes this even more apparent. Earlier in the Creed we affirm that Jesus is the only Son of the Father, that he was conceived by the Holy Spirit, and born of the Virgin Mary. Later in the Creed, we affirm that Jesus ascended into heaven, sits at the right hand of the Father, and will come again in glory to judge the living and the dead. When both the larger and more immediate

---

1. *Catechism of the Catholic Church*, nos. 194, 196.

textual contexts are put together, the narrative structure of Christ's redemptive plan looks something like this: incarnation—suffering—death—*descent into hell*—resurrection—ascent to the Father's right hand—return in glory—final judgment. Along with the resurrection, Jesus's descent into hell lies at the very center of the narrative movement of human redemption. It is the last action of Jesus's redemptive self-emptying and the point from which his transformation and glorious ascent begins.

Formulation and Truth

At this point in our inquiry, some pivotal questions arise. What is the correspondence between the statements contained in the Apostles' Creed and the truths they express? Is the narrative movement of Jesus's redemptive mission meant to be taken literally? Does it intend to reveal certain truths about the nature of Christ's redemptive action that can be removed from their present theological formulations in the hope of uncovering deeper, even more penetrating insights into the mystery of the Christ event? Is it possible to uncover the underlying truths of the Creed without doing damage to the tradition by which those truths have been passed down?

There are no simple answers to these important and enigmatic questions. Some of the statements in the Creed are affirmations of historical fact and require a close connection between the formulations themselves and the truths they bring to light. To say that Jesus suffered, died, and was buried, for example, leaves little room for discussion. Either these affirmations happened or they did not. The historical events to which they refer must be either accepted or denied.

Other statements in the Creed, however, are affirmations of faith that cannot be historically verified and thus offer more leeway in distinguishing between their formulations and the truths they disclose. To say that Jesus rose from the dead or ascended into heaven allows for some latitude about how these formulations should be understood. What do we mean, for example, when we say someone has risen from the dead? What is our understanding of ascension? What is our understanding of heaven? Unlike the notions of suffering, death, and burial, these concepts have no historical precedents with which to compare them.

Given this broad spectrum of possibilities, theologians need to discern with care the nature of the particular creedal statement before them and then determine to the best of their ability the relationship between the formulation itself and the truth it seeks to uncover. While a certain logical gap will probably always exist between the formulation and the truth to which it points, the precise extent of that gap will likely vary from one doctrinal formulation to the next.

Understanding Jesus's Descent

Like the doctrines of Jesus's resurrection and ascension into heaven, the creedal affirmation of Jesus's "descent into hell" allows for a certain amount of distance between its theological formulation and the truth it expresses. After all, there must be more to this doctrine than the image it conjures in our minds of a literal, spatial descent by Christ into a dark and gloomy underworld, a notion tied more to a now outdated Hebrew world view than the astonishing message of God's undying love for the world. Most would agree that hell is not so much a *place* of eternal damnation as a *state of being* that makes one completely alienated from God. In our reinterpretation of hell, the focus should be primarily on the spiritual and mental rather than an overemphasis on the physical. When speaking about Jesus's "descent into hell" today, perhaps it would be more appropriate to interpret it in a way that reveals something significant about humanity's primal experience of being alienated from God and about Jesus's central role in bringing that alienation to an end.

Alienation makes us feel isolated from ourselves, one another, and God. It hinders us in our journey through life and prevents us from becoming the persons we are called to become. Ronald Rolheiser puts it this way: "We are social beings, meant to live in love and intimacy with others. Our nature demands this. When, for whatever reasons, we cannot achieve this and communicate love as we should, then something is missing inside of us—and we feel it! We feel estranged and alienated."[2] To be in hell is to be in a state of complete and utter alienation from God. In such a state, we have lost complete touch with ourselves and, as a result, have become incapable of reaching out in love to anyone.

If we are honest, all of us will admit to having experienced, at some point in our lives, this sense of being estranged from and "out of sync" with ourselves, the world around us, and the God who created us. We feel at war with ourselves, divided within yet incapable of healing that division. Although we are conscious of it in different ways and in varying degrees, this sense of alienation is not a matter of personal choice (although choice can contribute to it), but a part of our existential condition as human beings. What makes matters worse is that we somehow sense that it was not meant to be this way, that something has gone terribly wrong with our human condition and that somehow

---

2. Rolheiser, *Restless Heart*, 43.

humanity as a whole bears at least some (if not all) responsibility for it.

Making All Things New

Christianity is all about how God chose to make things right again by sharing our human condition and overcoming this deeply ingrained sense of alienation lurking deep in our hearts. Down through the ages, the church has developed the doctrines of original sin and redemption to explain this universal sense of alienation and reveal the way God has chosen to rectify it.

Jesus's descent into hell is intimately tied to these fundamental Christian doctrines, each of which, like two sides of a coin, cannot exist without the other. Here, too, a distinction must be made between the formulations of these doctrines and the truths they disclose. Like Jesus's descent into hell, these doctrines allow room for interpretation. At its core, the doctrine of original sin affirms that all of humanity has somehow become alienated from God deep within its collective soul. The doctrine of redemption, in turn, affirms that, for any healing to take place, Jesus must enter that realm of alienation and preach the Good News of God's love for each and every human being. When seen in this light, Jesus's descent into hell is the final stage of his process of redemptive self-emptying. He has entered our world, given himself to us completely, to the point of dying for us, and even to the point of telling those who live in a state of complete alienation from the divine that God still loves them. Through the cross, Jesus reveals his message of divine compassion, breaks down the resistance of our primal alienation, and offers newness of life to all who would have it.

An example from Byzantine iconography illustrates this point very well. When depicting the descent into hell, the artist normally has Jesus standing on the toppled gates of hell with a scroll in one hand and pulling Adam out of a deep bottomless pit with the other. Below Adam, angels can be seen locking Satan and his dominions in chains that will hold them captive for all eternity. According to the principles of iconography, a scroll typically represents the preaching of the Word. Since "Adam," in Hebrew, means "man," in the universal sense of the term, what today many would refer to as "humanity," Jesus's lifting of Adam, the first man, indicates the healing of humanity's primal wounds and its elevation to even great heights through Christ's redeeming grace.[3]

The Word preached by Jesus to those in hell boldly proclaims a new creation made possible by his rising from the dead. Through his resurrection, Jesus, the firstfruits of the new humanity, takes fallen humanity by the hand, lifts it out of its primal state of alienation, and gives it the capacity to participate in a union with the divine more intimate than ever before thought possible. Jesus's descent into hell cannot be properly understood apart from his rising from the dead. It relates to the resurrection as the doctrine of original sin relates to the redemption. They, too, are like two sides of a coin: one depends on and cannot exist without the other.

Some Further Insights

The above presentation offers a creative rethinking of the church's traditional teaching of Jesus's descent into hell. What follows are a number of remarks designed to fill out this interpretation in practical and relevant ways.

3. Weier, *Festal Icons of the Lord*, 41–44.

Jesus and the Last Things

To begin with, this presentation challenges us to examine our minds and hearts in order to affirm what we truly believe about our faith. The doctrines of Christianity developed over time out of the experience of God's people and must always seek to speak to their ongoing experience. If they fail to do so, then these doctrines run the risk of becoming nothing but brittle assertions from the past that fail to inspire and give life. The challenge for today's believers is to engage these doctrines in such a way that they continue to speak to their experience, while all the while remaining faithful to the insights of our Christian forbearers. This presentation of Jesus's descent into hell uses different interpretive lenses to affirm the underlying truths of the traditional teaching so that they will be able to speak to the shifting contours of today's spiritual landscape.

A fundamental presupposition of this presentation is that it is possible to draw a distinction between a particular formulation of the Christian faith and the underlying truths it seeks to express. Since the complex relationship between language and meaning can be difficult to unravel (if at all), we have urged here that, when seeking a reformulation of a doctrine that would be more palatable to contemporary tastes, we proceed strictly on a case by case basis. The approach used in reinterpreting Jesus's descent into hell, for example, would not necessarily work in a discussion of other creedal statements, especially those with more historically verifiable claims.

Be that as it may, the distinction between a theological formula and the truth it discloses can be upheld on the basis of the analogy of human language. As with language, the Apostles' Creed is a complex system of symbols that seeks to convey an intricate web of meaning. While it is true that any translation of that meaning from one language to another is itself an interpretation (some of which are better than others), we maintain that translations are not only possible but, at times, absolutely required. This claim is all the more true for the church's proclamation of the gospel which, at one and the same time, must remain faithful to the apostolic tradition and relevant to the spiritual needs of each generation.

The choice of the phrase "alienation from the divine" as the existential equivalent to the Christian doctrine of hell has much in its favor. The term "alienation" is commonly used by many spiritual writers today and, when taken to its extreme, conveys a sense of the intense pain and isolation experienced in a life marked by a total absence of God. The knowledge, moreover, that there are different degrees of alienation (i.e., from simple non-inclusion to total estrangement) brings new insights into the Catholic doctrine of purgatory. If hell is the state of being in which an individual has become so alienated from God that he or she can no longer open his or her heart to God's compassionate love, then purgatory represents that state of being where a person's alienated heart is still capable of being moved to conversion. When seen in this light, the final judgment is not an external ruling exercised by Christ at the end of time, but the simple recognition of the cumulative effect of a person's choices in life on his or her heart.

Finally, Jesus's death on the cross, his descent into hell, and his resurrection from the dead do not bring an end to humanity's existential condition of alienation from the divine, but begin the process of its ongoing healing. Jesus's descent into hell was not a single, one-time event, but a continuous historical process of engaging humanity's alienation from the divine. Because his redemptive action is rooted both in and out of time, Jesus continues to empty himself for us to this very day by descending into the throes of our alienation from God in order to transform it and make of it a new creation. What has changed for us as a result of his redemptive action is that, in the midst of this alienation, each of us can now hear a still small voice echoing up from deep within our hearts, calling each of us by name and affirming God's compassionate and abounding love for us. That voice is the Spirit, the bond of love between the Father and the Son, who wishes not only to speak, but also to dwell within our hearts. Jesus's redemptive action makes it possible for each of us to live a life in the Spirit. His descent into hell is a stark reminder of what our lives would be like without him.

While these observations in no way exhaust the insights that this interpretation of Jesus's descent into hell has to offer, they demonstrate the extent to which such a presentation of the doctrine can be both continuous with the past, yet relevant to the spiritual sensitivities of today's believers.

Conclusion

In this chapter, we have seen what the doctrine of Jesus's descent into hell might look like once its underlying truths have been removed from the teaching's classical formulation and reinterpreted in a way that addresses the spiritual sensitivities of today's faithful. In doing so, we have seen that this descent is another way of speaking about Jesus's proclamation of the truth of his resurrection even to those who have completely alienated themselves from the divine love.

Although God's love for humanity is deep and plentiful, Jesus was well aware that not everyone would be ready to accept his message of forgiveness and intimate friendship with the divine. He experienced rejection during his public ministry and fully expected the same (if not worse) when he journeyed to hell after his gruesome and bloody death by crucifixion. This knowledge, however, did not prevent him from proclaiming his transforming message of God's love in the realm of the dead. On the contrary, it emboldened him all the more.

The fundamental point of this chapter is that this shadowy realm lies not in some dark, murky Sheol beneath the pillars of the earth, but deep in the confines of the human heart. Even today, Jesus goes there to proclaim his message and bring an end to humanity's primal alienation from God. Although the message he preaches is a source of vexation to many (hence the well-known phrase "harrowing of hell"), many whose hearts have not yet been completely hardened will listen to it and be moved to repentance.

In the final analysis, Jesus's descent into hell affirms that the Good News is destined to be proclaimed not just to all the ends of the earth, but to the heights and depths of reality itself, especially in the heights and depths of the human heart. "God is everywhere," as we learned from our penny catechism—even in hell! He is present not only by virtue of his power in keeping all things in being, but also by virtue of his Word and the healing message of hope he carries to our fallen and alienated humanity.

Reflection Questions

- What does the church mean when it says, "He descended into hell?"
- If hell represents the absence of God, then how can God go there?
- What does it mean to say that Jesus visited the dead?
- To what extent can the phrase mean that Jesus always reaches out to the alienated, both dead and alive?

- To what extent can it mean that he even reaches to those parts within your own heart that have become alienated from God and seemingly dead to God's transforming grace?

Prayer

Lord, you reach out to the alienated.
> Heal me of my isolation and loneliness.

3

The Judgment of Christ

For all of us must appear before the judgment seat of Christ, so that each may receive recompense for what has been done in the body, whether good or evil.

—2 COR 5:10

ACCORDING TO CATHOLIC BELIEF, Jesus Christ will return at the end of time in order to judge the world and establish the fullness of his kingdom.[1] As Catholics, we proclaim this message each Sunday when we gather for worship and together say: "He will come again in glory to judge the living and the dead, and his kingdom will have no end."[2] These words from the Nicene Creed remind us that human history is not open-ended but limited, finite, and drawing to a close. Just how this final consummation will take place is not for us to say. The Gospels themselves remind us of this very important truth: "But about that day or hour no one knows, neither the angels in heaven, nor the Son, but only the Father" (Mark 13:32).

1. *Catechism of the Catholic Church*, nos. 668–82.
2. *Roman Missal*, 511.

The Depths of Faith

This lack of knowledge concerning our human destiny should have an effect on the way we think and live in the present. It bids us to savor each moment of time, as if it might be our last. It also encourages us to take a good look at our lives and to put things in their proper perspective. Conversion, we are told, is ongoing. While we normally apply this insight to the moral dimensions of our faith, we also need to recognize its significance for specific doctrinal beliefs. The importance of this statement becomes all the more clear, once we recognize the intimate relationship existing between how we act and what we affirm about the nature of reality. If a gap exists between what we say with our lips and what we truly believe in our hearts, then there will most likely be a corresponding gap between the moral principles we publicly profess as a body of believers and the actual way we lead our lives. In the context of the church's doctrinal affirmation of the final judgment, we need to ask ourselves how deeply we believe in and are attached to it. Has our belief in it deepened over the years—or diminished? Do we ever think about its meaning? Does this belief mediate truth to us? Does it make sense to us any more? Does it inform our lives in any way? Or do we look upon it as a doctrinal holdover from a former age with little relevance for our present time, one that is best dealt with by giving it minimal notional assent or, worse yet, by simply ignoring it?

To be honest, I would have to admit that my outward actions do not always do justice to the implications of the Catholic doctrine of the last judgment. I say I believe it (and I do), but only half-heartedly. The teaching has little, if any, real bearing on the way I live my life. I cannot explain exactly why this is so. When I think about it, I am reminded

The Judgment of Christ

of H. Richard Niebuhr's somber assessment of late-nineteenth-century Protestant liberal theology: "A God without wrath brought men without sin into a kingdom without judgment through the ministrations of a Christ without a cross."[3] Niebuhr's statement hits home—at least for me. It touches an aspect of my ongoing predicament of faith and (I would assume) that of many others. It reflects a hidden, subliminal message that holds great sway over me and which, much to my dismay, I find myself actually backing up with my actions.

I am not saying that I have been overly influenced by the Protestant liberal mindset, although most American Catholics today have, to some extent, been culturally influenced by it and the values it promotes. This statement, however, has struck a chord within me about my own rendering of and accountability to the Catholic faith. It reminds me of how the various aspects of that faith are so interrelated. Everything in the faith is connected, to put it plainly, including all doctrinal truths. A subtle change in emphasis in one particular teaching will bring about a corresponding shift in many others. To sight just one example, a shift in our understanding of Jesus (for example, moving from a high to a low Christology) will have major ramifications for the way we understand the church and our role in it. That, in turn, affects the way we understand the church's relationship to the world and, by way of extension, of the world's relation to the kingdom. The point I am making is that a shift in just one aspect of our theological outlook will have a ripple effect on the whole.

---

3. Niebuhr, *Kingdom of God in America*, 193.

Jesus and the Last Things

A Paradigmatic Shift

It has now become commonplace to speak of the paradigmatic shift that took place in Catholic thought following the Second Vatican Council. The process of *aggiornamento* initiated by Pope John XXIII when calling the council spread through the church like wildfire. After centuries of maintaining a defensive, fortress mentality toward the world, the church encouraged Catholics to open up to the world and engage it in dialogue. To use another nomenclature coined by Niebuhr, the church came out of a "Christ against culture" understanding of its role in the world to a stance that looked to "Christ as the transformer of culture."[4]

This shift in attitude toward the world influenced the church's own self-understanding, especially with regard to its past. In their attempt to keep pace with the changes going on in the world and now, perforce, in the church, many of the Catholic faithful—clergy, religious, and laity alike—looked down upon or simply did away with many timely beliefs and practices that, after centuries of inclusion, had become an important part of their self-identity (for example, weekly confession, Friday abstinence, numerous private devotions). In the haste and enthusiasm of the moment, some got carried away and disregarded or at least assigned lesser significance to aspects of the faith that really should have remained central to Catholic spirituality.

With regard to the church's teaching on the final judgment, the popular post-Vatican II shift from a high Christology (emphasizing Christ's divinity more than his humanity) to a low Christology (emphasizing his humanity more than his divinity) brought about a similar shift in emphasis regarding Christ's action in the world. Rather than focusing on Christ's dominion and Lordship over heaven

4. See Niebuhr, *Christ and Culture*, 45–82, 190–229.

and earth, the shift to a low Christology emphasized Jesus's solidarity with and love for humanity. Jesus became more of a friend and brother than a lawgiver and judge; someone to whom we could turn in time of need rather than someone to hide from for fear of the punishment of our sins.

Such a shift in emphasis was healthy and good, but only within certain limits. To call Jesus our friend and brother is certainly a welcome change from the exaggerated adulation accorded to him during the years immediately preceding the council. But along with this change also came an imaginal misconstruing of Jesus's person and mission. Is not calling Jesus our friend and brother another confining stereotype? Can we honestly say that it fully captures the fullness of his life and message? Decades later, the delicate balance between the divine and human elements in Christ still remains out of sync in the popular Catholic imagination, so much so that one has to wonder if the change in attitude toward Christ that came about in the aftermath of Vatican II succeeded only in replacing one false image of God with another.

False God to False God

Over forty years ago, J. B. Phillips, an Anglican minister best known for his translation of the New Testament into modern English, wrote a book entitled, *Your God Is Too Small*. In it, he attempts: ". . . first to expose the inadequate conceptions of God which still linger unconsciously in many minds and which prevent our catching a glimpse of the true God; and secondly to suggest ways in which we can find the real God for ourselves."[5]

---

5. Phillips, *Your God Is Too Small*, 8–9.

Jesus and the Last Things

Phillips states that there are many false images of God that people possess and find very hard to shake. God can be thought of as a resident policeman, a demanding parent, a grand old man, a meek-and-mild companion, the embodiment of perfection, a heavenly lover, a managing director, a pale Galilean, a projected image, and assorted combinations of these and other stereotypes.[6] He concludes that, in order to have an adequate understanding of the divine, we must recognize that God, while infinitely beyond the powers of human comprehension, planned a concrete focusing of himself in the person of Jesus Christ.[7] Jesus alone reveals the mystery of God to us. To find God in our lives we must encounter this person and allow him to show us the true way of living. What does this mean concretely?

Our faith tells us that Jesus Christ is fully human *and* fully divine. If this is so, then we should relate to him as such and do all we can to ensure that he exists that way in our active imagination. To emphasize Christ's divinity at the expense of his humanity—or vice versa—is merely to substitute one false image of God for another. While the church has been careful to maintain this delicate balance in its doctrinal expressions, it has not always been successful in holding together this important "coincidence of opposites" in the popular imagination. Prior to the Second Vatican Council, Catholic piety and devotion tended to accentuate the divinity of Christ over his humanity. In the decades following the council, the reverse emphasis took precedence. At the dawn of the new millennium, we have been called to strike down our false images of Christ so that we can have a more adequate understanding of God's presence in our lives. We can do so, however, only by giving both Christ's divinity *and* his humanity a proper place in our hearts.

6. Phillips, *Your God Is Too Small*, 15–59.
7. Phillips, *Your God Is Too Small*, 120–24.

The Judgment of Christ

Contemplating the Face of Christ

In *Novo Millennio Ineuente*, his apostolic letter on the church in the third millennium, Saint John Paul II emphasizes the importance of prayer for the future of the church, especially contemplative prayer. He bids Christians the world over to contemplate the face of Christ so that the Spirit of Christ might touch and inspire them to follow the way of love.[8]

When we contemplate that face, the false images we have of God gradually break up and lose their hold over us. Jesus dispels our stereotypes and reveals to us the power of the divine in the fullness of his humanity. This happens by means of a mutual, reciprocal gaze. It begins when we open our hearts to him in prayer and become still in his presence. We look into his eyes and allow him to look into ours. We peer into his soul, and he peers into ours. We get to know him, and he gets to know us. In the midst of this stillness, we experience Jesus in the depths of our hearts. We gaze upon his humanity and touch the mystery of his divinity. He, in turn, gazes upon our humanity and sees there the person each of us is destined to become.

In the Gospel of John, Jesus refers to himself as "the light of the world" (John 9:5). He dispels the darkness from our hearts and enables us to see ourselves for who we really are. The church's teaching on the last judgment must be seen through the lens of this important scriptural saying. Christ brings to light all that is secret, all the hidden betrayals, all the subtle compromises, and all the self-deceptions that have crept into our lives over the years. When we contemplate the face of Christ, the light of his truth penetrates every fiber of our being and enables us to peer into the deepest recesses of our hearts. We are able to see things as they really are. Judgment, in this sense, is nothing more

---

8. John Paul II, *Novo Millennio Ineuente*, nos. 16–28.

than bringing to light our deepest aspirations. We spend our whole lives cultivating these hopes. Once revealed, we are free to respond as we wish. We chose to walk either toward or away from Christ. The grace to do so is his; the choice is entirely our own.

True Judgment, False Judgment

With regard to the final judgment, the Catholic imagination in recent decades has been subjected to the influence of opposing extremes. Prior to the Second Vatican Council, our emphasis on the divinity and Lordship of Christ brought the threat of judgment to the fore of Catholic spirituality. When combined with false images of God that presented him as an exacting taskmaster who kept a full account of our sins and who would demand a complete reckoning at the end of time, this emphasis made us deeply afraid of both God (for fear of what he might do to us) and of living life (for fear of making a mistake).

After Vatican II, this false notion of final judgment was gradually replaced by an equally false and misconceived perception. God, the vengeful judge, was replaced by a God who closes his eyes or simply looks the other way. Somehow during the course of the post-Vatican II era, many of the Catholic faithful—clergy, religious, and laity (including myself, I might add)—have managed to put the church's teaching on the final judgment so far back on the back burner of Catholic spirituality that it now has little, if any, vital and lasting impact on their lives. With no concrete assessment of human action on the horizon of human destiny, the ethical quality of our actions diminishes and can easily veer in the direction of moral relativism. The question facing us today is how we can strike both false images from the popular consciousness of Catholic spirituality and

THE JUDGMENT OF CHRIST

put a more balanced understanding of final judgment in its place.

To my mind, one of the best explanations of the Christian doctrine of the last judgment appears in C. S. Lewis's *The Great Divorce*. Written over seventy years ago, this imaginative fantasy describes in fine detail a chartered bus ride from hell to heaven. The travelers on this bus are free to make this trip at regular intervals from a dismal grey town deep in the underworld. Those making the excursion come out of a small crack in a rock and suddenly find themselves in a much larger world just on the outskirts of heaven. Finding themselves in a place where they are less real than the world around them, they feel like phantoms and find it hard to walk on the grass and gravel pathways of this deeper (and more real) arrangement of time and space. When they look around and talk to those who have been sent to meet them, they come to different conclusions about how to proceed. Some decide to make an even more arduous journey to God, who lives far away beyond distant mountains. Others decide to return to hell because they find it too painful to continue. Others never even get on the bus in the first place. Instead they decide to isolate themselves from human contact by wandering further and further into the lonely reaches of hell. Before long, they are great distances from the bus stop that offers them a glimpse of this other world. Eventually, even the knowledge of the existence of the bus stop for heaven is lost to their memory. A dialogue between one of the passengers who took the trip and a guide sent to meet him at the outskirts of heaven goes like this:

> "But I don't understand. Is judgment not final? Is there really a way out of Hell into Heaven?"
>
> "It depends on the way ye're using the words. If they leave that grey town behind it will not have been Hell. To any that leaves it,

> it is Purgatory. And perhaps ye had better not call this country Heaven. Not *Deep Heaven*, ye understand." (Here he smiled at me). "Ye can call it the Valley of the Shadow of Life. And yet to those who stay here it will have been Heaven from the first. And ye can call those sad streets in the town yonder the Valley of the Shadow of Death: but to those who remain there they will have been in Hell even from the beginning."[9]

Lewis achieves through narrative what the church has forgotten how to do through its doctrinal formulations—capture the Christian imagination! He does so by writing a story that collapses eternity into a space-time continuum and develops the various thought processes that lead the characters in the story to decide things the way they do. Central to his presentation is the mysterious interplay between human freedom and divine grace. Those who make the journey to Deep Heaven can do so only with help from above. Those who do not make it simply refuse this help and decide to go their own way. When viewed in this light, final judgment is more a matter of personal choice than of divine rejection. People are permitted to judge for themselves, to make their own decisions about things of ultimate value. God allows us to choose our own destiny. The doctrine of final judgment reminds us of the power of human choice and its capacity to reject even passionate and loving overtures of the living God.

Conclusion

The next time we recite the Creed at Sunday Mass and come to the words about Christ coming again in glory to judge the living and the dead, perhaps we should pause and

9. Lewis, *Great Divorce*, 66–67.

ask ourselves how firmly we hold that belief and what it really means to us. For too long, the Catholic imagination has lost touch with the powerful truth about humanity's final destiny. We have become lazy practitioners of the faith, allowing the doctrinal truths of our religion to pass readily from our lips before resounding deep in our hearts. Rather than simply settling for the way things are or, perhaps even worse, reverting to the false understanding of final judgment in vogue in an earlier period in time, we need to find ways of sparking our imagination today so that the truths of the faith, mysterious and difficult to comprehend as they may be, can penetrate our hearts and minds and guide us boldly and assuredly in our journey to Deep Heaven.

Reflection Questions

- What is the difference between true judgment and false judgment?
- How have false images of God affected your understanding of the meaning and purpose of the last judgment?
- Do you agree that a person's actions in this life affect his or her eternal destiny?
- "A God without wrath brought men without sin into a kingdom without judgment through the ministrations of a Christ without a cross." Do you agree?
- How can the Catholic imagination get back in touch with the powerful truth about humanity's final destiny?

Prayer

Lord, you will come to judge the living and the dead.
   Have mercy on me when I stand before you.

4

The Destiny of Christ

"Do not let your hearts be troubled. Believe in God, believe also in me. In my Father's house there are many dwelling places. If it were not so, would I have told you that I go to prepare a place for you? And if I go and prepare a place for you, I will come again and will take you to myself, so that where I am, there you may be also. And you know the way to the place where I am going."

—John 14:1–4

In the opening verses of the Farewell Discourse of John's Gospel, Jesus tells his disciples that there are "many dwelling places" in his Father's house (John 14:2). Over the centuries, this phrase has been interpreted in a number of ways, from a literal, spatial understanding of heaven on one side of the spectrum to an esoteric presentation of various degrees of raised consciousness on the other. Even today, its precise meaning eludes the careful scrutiny of many New Testament exegetes.

It is not easy to pinpoint the meaning of this phrase. Jesus is employing a metaphor, seemingly to emphasize the eschatological consequences of his relationship with the Father for his followers. The original intention behind a metaphor, however, is not always easy to understand; neither is the added significance it might acquire over time. I propose to offer here a simple pastoral interpretation of the phrase, one that remains faithful to the best that New Testament exegesis has to offer, while at the same time seeking to find relevant points of contact for today's believers.

Some Important Background

To get a sense of the meaning of the phrase, "many dwelling places," we must first try to discover how it stands in relationship to the one immediately following it, "in my Father's house." The connection between the two is important. Ancient Near Eastern literature usually took the image of the "Father's house" as a reference to heaven.[1] This metaphor is based on a projection of human experience onto the level of the divine. If people reside in houses, then so must God; the human is considered but a faint reflection of the divine plane.

The danger in such a facile projection from the human sphere onto the divine is the tendency to identify the two or, to be even more precise, to collapse the higher level into the lower. Although this danger was certainly avoided in the more learned circles of Jesus's day, one wonders if it was so for the masses, especially given their limited world view and the vagaries of the popular imagination. For this reason, we must be careful when imagining heaven as a physical place with spatial dimensions similar to our present earthly experience. Jesus came to build a *new* heaven

---

1. See Perkins, "Gospel according to John," 974.

The Destiny of Christ

and a *new* earth, not merely to remodel or reshape the presently existing ones.

What then can be said about the meaning of the phrase, "in my Father's house"? Even today, Jesus's metaphor is still pregnant with meaning. A house is, first and foremost, a setting for living where relationships take root and develop. When Jesus talks about his "Father's house," he is really referring to the intimate relationship he shares with the Father. When he says that there are many dwelling places there, he is telling his disciples that they too can share in the intimate love of the Father.[2]

How is this so? The answer is clear for the Gospel writer: Jesus's selfless self-offering has made it possible for the God to inhabit the human heart. Why does God wish to dwell there? The answer is "Love." For the Gospel writer, no other explanation suffices: God is deeply in love with humanity and wishes to befriend it. Because we have been created in his image and likeness, God wishes to draw all of us into an intimate sharing of his divine love. He does not want to call us "servants," but "friends" (John 15:15). To show his love for us, he became one of us and gave his life for us in a horrible death: "No one has greater love than this, to lay down one's life for one's friends" (John 15:13).

Friendship with God

Jesus's death on the cross was a compelling demonstration of God's love for humanity. Through it, the Father demonstrated the extent he was willing to go in order to penetrate the human heart with his divine compassion. He gave up his only begotten Son, who freely handed himself over to death. Jesus lived in close communion with his Father and

2. See Blank, *Gospel according to John*, 53–55.

pointed out the way to him for his disciples: "I am the way, and the truth, and the life. No one comes to the Father except through me" (John 14:6). Jesus died so that we might have life and have it in abundance.

Saint Alphonsus Liguori puts it a slightly different way: "The paradise of God," he says, "is the heart of man."[3] To inhabit our hearts is God's deepest desire, his notion of holy bliss. Jesus made it possible for God to dwell in the human heart and for humanity to dwell in the heart of God. This mutual indwelling lies at the very core of the divine friendship Jesus offers his disciples: ". . . I have called you friends, because I have made known to you everything that I heard from my Father" (John 15:15).

Also important for understanding the meaning of the phrase are the words of Jesus appearing immediately before it: "Do not let your hearts be troubled. Believe in God, believe also in me" (John 14:1). The call to courage and the call to faith open Jesus's Farewell Discourse and preface his remarks about the many dwelling places in his Father's house. If Jesus promises his disciples that he will go ahead to prepare a place for them and even return to lead them there (John 14:2–3), he will do so only if they have the faith and courage to carry on without him for a time. Jesus's promised return is a clear reference to his second coming, a cataclysmic event which many early Christians believed was imminently approaching and would take place in their own lifetimes.

When seen in this light, Jesus speaks about the dwelling places in his Father's house in order to enkindle in his disciples' hearts a hope that will carry them through the difficult times ahead. Yes, he must leave them for a time, but he promises to return and to take them with him. In his Farewell Discourse, Jesus is taking leave of his disciples,

---

3. Liguori, *Way to Converse Always*, 395.

but also encouraging them to face the future with undying faith and steadfast courage. He also is telling them that he is not really leaving them, but merely accompanying them on their journey in another form and under another guise. He is reminding them that he will always be with them, residing in their hearts, just as the Father resides in his heart and he in the Father's.[4]

Many Dwelling Places

The above explanation makes it clear that Jesus uses the metaphor of many dwelling places in his Father's house to offer his disciples a share in his intimate relationship with the Father. This means that heaven is not primarily about a place or some higher level of consciousness, but relationships.

There are many dwelling places in the Father's house because each person's relationship with God is unique and cannot be replicated. Each relationship reveals something special about God and about the person. If that relationship did not exist, a part of God that we could have known would remain a mystery to us, and we would be all the poorer for it.

There are many dwelling places in the Father's house because the Father's heart is infinitely deep and full of unbounded love, making him able to love each individual as though he or she were the only person in existence. All of these dwelling places are connected and lead to deeper relationships not only with God, but also with one another. When seen in this light, the communion of saints is not a bland collection of homogeneous relationships, but a vibrant celebration of life in the Living God.

---

4. See Blank, *Gospel according to John*, 66–67.

There are many dwelling places in the Father's house, because that is exactly the way the Father wants it. It has often been said that "Good is self-diffusive" (i.e., "self-giving").[5] The same is true for Love. God simply cannot contain his love for us. He loves by nature, and cannot do otherwise. Even so, he loves us freely and with great generosity. He calls each of us by name and invites us to enter into an intimate friendship with him. To do so, he gives us time to get to know and befriend him. He does not force his love upon us, but wishes us to turn to him freely and of our own accord.

There are many dwelling places in the Father's house because that is precisely what we need as human beings: a place where we can be ourselves, a place we can call our own, a place we can call home. Our true home is to rest in the Father's heart. Saint Augustine put it so well, ". . . you have made us for yourself, and our hearts are restless until they find peace in you."[6] We were made for intimate friendship with God. That is what we yearn for. That is what we long for. The dwelling places of which I speak are first and foremost places of rest.

Some Further Insights

Given the above, this phrase from John's Gospel carries with it a number of important pastoral implications.

If heaven is primarily about relationships, and especially the one we share with the Father, then it enters our midst whenever we form genuine bonds of love with God and those around us. The coming of the kingdom of God is not something that we project onto the distant and uncertain

---

5. See, for example, Aquinas, *Summa Theologica* (1.5.4), 25–26; Pseudo-Dionysius, *Divine Names* (4:20), 86–88.

6. Augustine of Hippo, *Confessions* (1.1), 17.

future, but a living reality that, with God's help, we are now in the process of constructing. Those involved in ministry need to find ways of helping the people they serve to look for the presence of the kingdom in their midst. The gospel metaphor of "many dwelling places" in the Father's house is one way of doing so.

In today's postmodern culture, there is a temptation to interpret this gospel metaphor in a relativistic manner. The "many places" in the Father's house is said to demonstrate the shifting boundaries of truth and the conviction that beliefs themselves ultimately matter very little in the shaping of our destiny. The relational explanation of the metaphor offered here addresses the spiritual sensitivities of the postmodern world, but firmly rejects such a relativistic viewpoint. Those involved in ministry can use this metaphor to meet people where they are, yet also proclaim the Gospel message that truth is not relative, but rooted in the life and person of Jesus.

Similarly, the current mindset of Western culture might lead some to interpret the gospel metaphor in an overly individualistic fashion. From this point of view, the "many dwelling places" of the Father's house are seen to exist in isolation from each other, as if they were individual mansions (even fortresses) with little if anything to do with one another. The relational interpretation of the metaphor counteracts this misplaced notion and offers a fundamentally communal understanding of the meaning of "fullness of life in God." Those involved in ministry can use the metaphor to instruct those they serve to value this emphasis on the social nature of beatitude and the need for the practice of an authentic "spirituality of communion."

This gospel metaphor should help Christians to recognize the normative value of Jesus's love for the Father for their own faith. At the same time, it should also lead them to examine the images that pass through their mind when they think of or pray to God. Jesus's word, "Abba, Father," was a deep sign of affection, one that Christians the world over are called to share in. It was never meant to limit God, however, and should never be used as such. Those involved in ministry can use the gospel metaphor of the "Father's house" to help those they serve examine what their images of God really are. Only by identifying these images and naming them will they be able to separate the true ones from the false ones.

Finally, this relational interpretation of this gospel metaphor offers Christians a deeper insight into the mutual indwelling of Jesus and the Father and the way each of us can share in this reality. The bond between Jesus and the Father is the Spirit. Because of Jesus's death, that same Spirit can now dwell in our own hearts. Those in ministry can use this gospel metaphor as a way of talking about the beauty of the God's desire to commune with us in this way. The metaphor offers us a way of speaking of the importance of nurturing in our lives a spirituality of the heart rooted in Jesus's promise of lasting friendship with the divine.

Conclusion

The gospel metaphor of the "many dwelling places" in the Father's house still captures the imagination. We may find ourselves interpreting it in any number of ways. Some of these interpretations may be ill-conceived (perhaps even harmful) to our faith. Others will give us cause for reflection and, on a good day, even inspire us. The point of this chapter is that there is a way of understanding the meaning of this potent gospel metaphor that is both faithful to current New Testament scholarship and relevant to the spiritual sensitivities of today's believers. Even more importantly, we have shown that the metaphor offers some very concrete and practical pastoral insights.

When searching through the Scriptures, those involved in ministry need to keep an eye out for valid parallels between the New Testament faith and the faith of those they serve. The metaphor of the "many dwelling places" offers one such point of contact. When understood as an invitation to enter into an intimate relationship with the divine, one that preserves the uniqueness of that relationship for each individual, yet also relishes its importance for the community of believers, it offers today's believers a way of addressing some of the deepest yearnings of their hearts. For this reason alone, the message it bears needs to be shared with others. If nothing else, it will impart a different sense of what it means for God's kingdom to be in our midst and in our hearts. It will also help us to recognize all the more why we should earnestly pray for the coming of that kingdom and the fullness of life it promises.

Reflection Questions

- How do you picture heaven? How is it continuous with this present reality? How does it differ?
- Do you believe your relationship with God is unique and cannot be replicated?
- What does heaven have to do with experiencing friendship with God?
- What does Jesus mean when he says there are many mansions in his Father's house?
- Do you believe that heaven for God is to dwell in the human heart?

Prayer

Lord, help me make my way to heaven.
> Help me find my place in your Father's house.

5

The Four Last Things

Then I saw a new heaven and a new earth; for the first heaven and the first earth had passed away, and the sea was no more. And I saw the holy city, the new Jerusalem, coming down out of heaven from God, prepared as a bride to meet her husband. And I heard a loud from the throne saying, "See, the home of God is among mortals. He will dwell with them; they will be his peoples, and God himself will be with them; he will wipe every tear from their eyes. Death will be no more; mourning and crying and pain will be no more, for the first things have passed away." And the one who was seated on the throne said, "See, I am making all things new."

—Rev 21:1–5

THE CHURCH'S TEACHING ON the last things has important implications for how we conduct our lives. By insisting that history is purposeful and moving towards an end, it asks us to examine our actions in the light of what awaits us both when we die and at the consummation of all things at the end of time. In doing so, it tells us that the particular ends for which we act should also be oriented toward our ultimate end in God. It strongly insists that only by putting this end first and keeping it there will we be able to keep our priorities straight and act in a manner that will lead us to our final destination. One of the traditional ways Christians did this was by meditating on the last things. This venerable devotional practice helped believers to stay focused on their ultimate end and to act in ways that would get them there. Through it, prayer and action became intimately related; Christian spirituality and morality, uniquely intertwined.

The Goal of Meditation

Christian meditation (*meditatio*) has been described as ". . . nothing else than an intimate sharing between friends; it means taking time frequently to be with Him who we know loves us."[1] It is a quiet, reflective, and affective pondering of the mysteries of the Christian faith. It is distinct from vocal prayer (*oratio*) since it is not spoken or verbalized in any way and from contemplation (*contemplatio*) since it involves the use of discursive thought rather than intuited and restful stillness in the divine presence.[2] During the course of the centuries, a number of methods of Christian meditation (or "mental prayer," as it is also called) have been developed.[3] All include a period of preparation, some reflection on a particular aspect of the faith, an application of that reflection to one's life, a resolution to do something about it, and a concluding prayer.[4] Meditation is so important for growth in the Christian life that some say it is "morally necessary for salvation," a phrase meaning

1. Teresa of Avila, *Life* (8.5), 67.
2. See Guardini, *Prayer in Practice*, 120–57.
3. See Lercaro, *Metodi di Orazione Mentale*, 5, 91, 120, 146, 171, 216.
4. See Aumann, *Spiritual Theology*, 322.

that, without it, a person would be able to make his or her way to God only with great difficulty.[5]

The principal goal of Christian meditation is intimacy with God. We enter into conversation with God in order to draw closer to him. This conversation requires solitude of heart and must take place against a backdrop of silence. When we meditate, we open our hearts to God and reveal to him our deepest and most pressing concerns. He, in turn, responds to us in and through the surrounding silence that penetrates our thoughts and innermost yearnings. Through this intimate dialogue, we eventually receive insights into our lives and the proper course of action we should take with respect to the problems and dilemmas facing us. We receive these insights so that we can act on them. If we fail to do so, then our meditation remains half-hearted and incomplete.

When we meditate, it is best to focus on those aspects of the faith that we find nourishing and life-giving. While these topics will vary from person to person, there will also very likely be a large number of areas shared in common. The mystery of Christ's passion, death, and resurrection, for example, lies at the very heart of the faith and offers all who meditate upon it the opportunity to enter more deeply into Christ's passage from death. The same is true for the mystery of the Eucharist, which allows us to gather in thanksgiving for the gift of Christ's body and blood. Meditating on the four last things—death, judgment, heaven, and hell—has also been very important for the spiritual life. When we fail to reflect on those things related to our final destiny, it is very easy for us to become distracted by lesser concerns and by thoughts and activities that might get in the way of our relationship with God.

---

5. See, for example, Liguori, *Mental Prayer*, 252–58.

JESUS AND THE LAST THINGS

A Shift in Focus

Over forty years ago, E. J. Fortman described the traditional Catholic teaching on the last things as follows: "(1) there is life after death in a disembodied condition for every human being until the general resurrection, and this involves a particular judgment at death, a temporary purgatory for some, a permanent hell and heaven and probably a permanent limbo; (2) at the Parousia of Christ there will be a general resurrection of all men, followed by everlasting life for all men either in heaven or hell."[6] This basic teaching is largely confirmed in the *Catechism of the Catholic Church*, although the teaching on "limbo" (*limbus puerorum*), a state of natural (as opposed to supernatural) bliss for children dying without baptism, is omitted. Instead, the *Catechism* simply entrusts these children to the mercy of God and encourages us to hope for their salvation.[7]

Although the traditional teaching on the last things has remained largely unchanged, the emphasis given to its various aspects has not. Prior to the Second Vatican Council, Catholic spirituality and popular devotion often emphasized the realities of sin, death, and judgment over the mercy and compassion of a loving God. The emphasis on these themes often gave rise to a deep-rooted anxiety among believers about their eternal destiny, causing them to practice their faith out of fear of judgment instead of love for God. Most people perceived holiness as a worthy but distant goal, one that only a precious few could ever hope to attain. Sanctity was an individual enterprise and beyond the reach of the mass of humanity. Suffering and purgation were the best that most people could hope for in this life and in the world to come.

6. Fortman, *Everlasting Life After Death*, ix.
7. See *Catechism of the Catholic Church*, nos. 1020–65, 1261.

Since the Second Vatican Council, however, God's mercy and compassion have taken the center stage of Catholic spirituality. The emphasis on sin, death, and judgment has given way to the universal call to holiness and the transformative powers of the Risen Lord.[8] The emphasis on these themes has fostered a deep-seated trust in God's love for humanity as a whole and for each human person. This focus on God's love has given rise to a Christian spirituality that is corporate in nature and that expresses love for God through love for one's neighbor. The concerns of the post-Vatican II Church for social justice, human solidarity, the common good, and the dignity of the human person flow directly from this important shift of emphasis in the church's eschatological teaching.

Finding a Balance

Although the above shift in emphasis has been a healthy remedy for the anxiety-ridden spirituality that had haunted many Catholic churches prior to the Second Vatican Council, one has to wonder if the Catholic faithful of post-Vatican II era might have unwittingly erred in the opposite direction. Could they have overreacted to the distorted spirituality they were experiencing? Could one exaggeration have possibly given way to another? Could this important shift in the popular Catholic mindset have led to the tacit omission of truths previously taken for granted? Could a "spirituality of fear" flowing from an almost exclusive emphasis on sin, death, and judgment have inadvertently given way to a "spirituality of presumption" that, for all the good it encourages in the lives of believers, also promotes little sense of sin or of God's loving discipline?

---

8. See Vatican Council II, *Lumen Gentium*, nos. 39–42.

Such questions arise not out of criticism, but from concern for the true spirit of Catholicism. However expressed, an authentic Catholic spirituality must seek to synthesize conflicting extremes in search of a balance that will do justice to the truths of the faith to which countless people have dedicated their lives. When dealing with the last things in the post-Vatican II era, the challenge before us is to remain faithful to official teaching of the church in a way that will steer free of either extremes of fear and presumption. To do so, the various facets of the church's eschatological teaching must be presented in concert with one another, and in a way that will enable believers to sense their close interrelation.

The Christian teaching on death, for example, cannot be properly understood apart from its teaching on the resurrection. Nor will its teaching on the particular and general judgments make sense apart from its teaching on the dignity of the human person, humanity's communal identity, and the purposeful movement of history. In a similar way, it would be important to distinguish among the four last things, those which are "last" from a strictly historical perspective (i.e., death as the end of earthly life and judgment as taking place at the end of time) and those which are "last" from the perspective of eternity (i.e., heaven and hell). Such distinctions will emphasize the "already-but-not-yet" character of the church's eschatological teaching and serve to bring out its important spiritual moral implications.

The Ethics of Eschatology

As Michael Simpson affirmed some forty years ago, "[a]ny attempt . . . to expound an ethical system must be eschatological, it cannot ignore the 'end' to which man is called."[9] He went on to emphasize the symbolic nature of the church's teaching on the last things and did so in a way that remained faithful to past formulations yet relevant to the spiritual sensitivities of his day. The following observations seek to continue this general line of thinking and to make relevant applications to the present circumstances of the post-Vatican II church.

God is humanity's ultimate end and all human action must somehow be oriented toward the divine. When our actions deviate from that end for no good reason, they lead us away from God and affect us on the level of human becoming. Because human action is an expression of human existence, our destiny is intimately tied to the choices we make in life. If we stray continuously from the path leading to God, we will neither find God nor reach our fullest potential as human beings. God is our ultimate end, unless we stubbornly insist on choosing another.

The process of humanity's divinization is closely related to its ultimate end in God. The beatific vision (i.e. *visio Dei*) for which we are destined means that we will one day be given the opportunity to see God face-to-face. For this to happen, however, God must first elevate us to a level of transformed existence capable of living in intimate fellowship with him. This process of transformation begins in this life in our walk of faith and manifests itself in our close cooperation with the power of divine love. Although the creator/creature distinction will always remain intact, the beatific vision intimately unites God's vision of us with our vision of God.

In light of the above, the four last things—death, judgment, heaven, and hell—represent a challenge to each person and to humanity as a whole to orient their lives entirely toward God. Together, they form part of the church's language

9. Simpson, *Death and Eternal Life*, 90.

of conversion that confronts us with the fundamental choice of accepting God's love and offer of intimate friendship or rejecting it. The choices we make in our daily lives and our entire destiny depend on this fundamental decision about the nature of our relationship with God.

The terms "death" and "judgment" confront us with the finite nature of our earthly sojourn and the infinite value assigned to our deliberated actions. As such, they represent the historical dimensions of the church's eschatological teaching, the part that looks upon the last things from the perspective of the spatio-temporal order. The finality of death and the necessary orientation of human action toward the eternal provide the broad general contours within which the principles of Christian morality reveal themselves and gradually unfold.

The terms "heaven" and "hell," by way of contrast, confront us with questions of our eternal destiny. They affirm the survival of human life after death through God's power to reconstitute and subsequently transform the human body and soul. They remind us that our lives on earth are moving toward one of two possible destinations: life with or without God. Although God desires to have an intimate and everlasting friendship with each of us, he cannot form such a relationship against our will. In the end, we are the ones who choose our final destiny. Our actions in life reveal that choice and ultimately put it into effect.

The "already-but-not-yet" quality of Christian eschatology has a direct influence on human action. Our actions in the world are rooted in the past, performed in the present, and oriented toward the future. They may contribute to the present realization of God's kingdom in our midst, but never do so completely. Each human action represents but a single point in a process of becoming that points beyond itself to something still to come. This aspect of human action demands that a human life be considered in its totality and not merely as a compilation of disjunctive and isolated acts. It also helps us to understand the church's doctrine of purgatory, which recognizes the dimension of incompleteness in human action and human life and allows for a state of cleansing or purgation after death so that the person might be further readied for his or her face-to-face encounter with the divine.

The church's teaching on the last things reminds us that human action is an expression of human existence and has a reconstituting effect on it. We shape ourselves over the course of our lives through the deliberate choices we make. At the end of our lives, it is impossible for us to undo what these choices have made of us. Only God can do so, and he will not do it if we refuse to allow him. Human action is not accidental to human existence, but flows from it and molds its outcome. The teaching emphasizes that each of us has but one life to live and that what we do determines who and what we become.

A balanced understanding of the church's teaching on the last things affirms that our deliberate choices should be made not out of fear or presumption, but as a loving response to Jesus, the Lord of history. The Christian message places Jesus at the center of human history and considers him both the model and the goal toward which all human action should tend. Our actions will carry us to our ultimate end in God, however, only if they are united with those of Jesus. Our participation in his resurrected life confers salvific value on our actions and enkindles in us the hope of one day seeing God face-to-face.

The church's teaching on the last things demonstrates the intimate relationship between Christian faith and action in the world. Every Christian doctrine has an ethical implication that flows from it—and vice versa. For eschatology, this means that the true goal of human action is to enable a person to become fully alive in the faith so that he or she will achieve the end for which he or she was made. The circular relationship between faith and action lies at the very heart of Christian ethics and should not be overlooked. Christian action in the world has a very specific purpose that makes it qualitatively different from other ethical systems.

Finally, the church's teaching on the last things also reveals the intimate connection between spirituality and morality. A "spirituality of fear" stemming from an eschatology based on an overemphasis on sin, death, and judgment results in fearful actions and attitudes toward God, neighbor, and the world. Similarly, a "spirituality of presumption" based on a simplistic and naïve image of God, as one who overlooks the face of evil and fails to discipline those he loves, results in irresponsible actions performed with little sense of their damaging consequences. In contrast to these exaggerated emphases, a balanced eschatological spirituality results in actions performed out of love for God, others, and the world he created.

Conclusion

Although the church's official teaching on the last things has changed little from pre- to post-Vatican II times, its reception and subsequent interpretation has at times given rise to misunderstandings. If a "spirituality of fear" rooted in exaggerated notions of sin, death, and judgment was operative in the period just prior to the council, a swing to the other extreme after the council unwittingly promoted a "spirituality of presumption" in the popular Catholic mindset. The challenge for Catholics today is to develop an integrated understanding of Christian eschatology that will spawn a balanced spirituality that responds to God and to the world around them not out of fear or presumption, but out of a desire to love God and to carry out his will.

An integrated understanding of the church's teaching on the last things has a great deal to do with the moral and spiritual life. It emphasizes the purposeful movement of history and of each human life. It presents the twofold possibilities regarding our eternal destiny, i.e., life with or without God. It points out the infinite dimensions of human decision-making and the consequences flowing from it. It acknowledges the incompleteness of our lives and allows for an intermediate state after death to ready us for our encounter with God. It asserts that God's love is stronger than evil, but can still be deliberately and resolutely refused.

The church's teaching on the last things insists on the importance of "putting last things first" in the lives of believers. It encourages us to meditate on death, judgment, heaven, and hell as way of confronting the finitude of human life and the orientation of our actions toward our final destiny. It reminds us of the nature of human action and the effect it has on human existence. It encourages us to hope in the coming of the kingdom and to help establish its presence in the here and now. The Apostle Paul reminds us that faith, hope, and love are the only things that last and that the greatest of these is love (1 Cor 13:13). The church's teaching on the last things affirms the primacy of love in the fabric of the universe. So strong is this love that it can reverse the natural processes of death and reunite what once was separated. It affirms that nothing can separate us from the love of God, nothing except our own unwillingness and stubborn resistance to change.

Reflection Questions

- How do death, judgment, heaven, and hell shape our outlook on life?
- Do they do this for better? For worse? Somewhere in-between?
- Why is it important to meditate on the four last things?
- How can we maintain a proper balance in our spirituality between the realities of sin, death, and judgment, on the one hand, and the mercy and compassion of a loving God, on the other?
- What happens to our outlook on life when the last things are not taken seriously or, worse yet, simple ignored?

Prayer

Lord, walk with me as I walk through life.
    Give me the courage and strength to follow you to the end.

Conclusion

Putting Last Things First

THE FOUR LAST THINGS—death, judgment, heaven, and hell—lie at the very heart of the Christian message. Jesus conquered death by the power of love. He judges humanity with compassion and a heart full of mercy. He promises his followers an eternity of joy in the Father's presence. He paints the dire consequences of those who freely reject the divine life he offers them. In this respect, the last things point to the one thing that matters: "You shall love the Lord your God with all your heart, and with all your soul, and with all your strength, and with all your mind; and your neighbor as yourself" (Luke 10:27). All else is secondary.

Jesus is the Alpha and Omega, the beginning and the end (Rev 22:13). He wants us to put last things first and first things last. For Catholics, the four last things all point to him. We die in him and hope in finding life after death (Death). We surrender ourselves to his discerning gaze and discover the truth about ourselves (Judgment). We enter into friendship with him and, through him, enjoy communion with the Father by the power of the Spirit (Heaven). We also know that we can freely choose to reject his love and suffer the dire consequences of living eternally alienated from the source of all life and love (Hell). With the Apostle Paul, we understand that Jesus offers us an eternity of mutual indwelling: "I have been crucified with Christ, and it is no longer I who live, but it is Christ who lives in me" (Gal 2:19–20). With him, we proclaim that the four last things ultimately converge in the proclamation of the Gospel of Love: "And now faith, hope, and love abide, these three; and the greatest of these is love" (1 Cor 13:13). This proclamation extends to the four corners of the earth and to the deepest, even the darkest recesses of the human heart. This proclamation, "God is love" (1 John 4:8) resounds throughout the entire universe and draws all things, even the final things, into humble love of a God who created us, who entered our world to redeem us, and who dwells within our hearts to sanctify us and to lead us safely home.

Bibliography

Aquinas, Thomas. *Summa Theologica*. Translated by the Fathers of the English Dominican Province. Allen, TX: Christian Classics, 1981.

Augustine of Hippo. *Confessions*. Translated by Rex Warner. New York: New American Library, 1963.

Aumann, Jordan. *Spiritual Theology*. London: Sheed and Ward, 1980.

Blank, Josef. *The Gospel According to John*. Translated by Matthew J. O'Connell. New Testament for Spiritual Reading 8. New York: Crossroad, 1981.

Bushnell, Horace. *The Vicarious Sacrifice*. London: Richard D. Dickinson, 1880.

Catechism of the Catholic Church. Rome: Libreria Editrice Vaticana, 1994.

Fortman, E. J. *Everlasting Life After Death*. New York: Alba, 1976.

Guardini, Romano. *Prayer in Practice*. Translated by Leopold of Loewenstein-Wertheim. New York: Pantheon, 1957.

Holy Bible: New Revised Standard Version with Apocrypha. New York: Oxford University Press, 1989.

John Paul II. *Novo Millennio Ineunte*. http://w2.vatican.va/content/john-paul-ii/en/apost_letters/2001/documents/hf_jp-ii_apl_20010106_novo-millennio-ineunte.html.

Lercaro, Giacomo. *Metodi di Orazione Mentale*. Genoa: Massimo, 1957.

Lewis, C. S. *The Great Divorce*. New York: Macmillan, 1946.

———. *The Problem of Pain*. New York: Macmillan, 1962.

Liguori, Alphonsus. *Mental Prayer and the Exercises of a Retreat*. In *The Complete Works of Saint Alphonsus de Liguori* 3, edited by Eugene Grimm, 252–378. Brooklyn: Redemptorist Fathers, 1927.

———. *The Way to Converse Always and Familiarly with God*. In *The Complete Works of Saint Alphonsus de Liguori* 2, edited by Eugene Grimm, 391–417. Brooklyn: Redemptorist Fathers, 1926.

Niebuhr, H. Richard. *Christ and Culture*. New York: Harper Torchbooks, 1956.

Bibliography

———. *The Kingdom of God in America*. New York: Harper & Brothers, 1937.

Perkins, Pheme. "The Gospel according to John." In *The New Jerome Biblical Commentary*, edited by Raymond E. Brown et al., 942–85. Upper Saddle River, NJ: Prentice-Hall, 1990.

Phillips, J. B. *Your God Is Too Small*. New York: Macmillan, 1967.

Pseudo-Dionysius. *The Divine Names*. In *Pseudo-Dionysius: The Complete Works*, 47–131. Translated by Colm Luibheid. New York: Paulist, 1987.

Rolheiser, Ronald. *The Restless Heart: Finding Our Spiritual Home in Times of Loneliness*. New York: Doubleday, 2004.

The Roman Missal. English Translation according to the Third Typical Edition. Italy: Magnificat, 2011.

Simpson, Michael. *Death and Eternal Life*. Hales Corners, WI: Clergy, 1971.

Teresa of Avila. *Life*. In *The Collected Works of Saint Teresa of Jesus*, vol. 1, 1–308. Translated by Kieran Kavanaugh and Otilio Rodriguez. Washington, DC: ICS, 1976.

Vatican Council II. *Lumen Gentium*. In *Vatican Council II: The Conciliar and Post Conciliar Documents*, edited by Austin Flannery, 350–426. Collegeville, MN: Liturgical, 1992.

Weier, M. Helen. *Festal Icons of the Lord*. Collegeville, MN: Liturgical, 1977.

www.ingramcontent.com/pod-product-compliance
Lightning Source LLC
Chambersburg PA
CBHW051706090426
42736CB00013B/2564